A Whale of a Wish!

Written by Razana Noor

Illustrated by Rahima Begum

ISBN: 978-9948-13-544-9

For J – motivator, critic and babysitter extraordinaire!
Thank you for EVERYTHING!

There was once a young whale, as kind as can be
Living with his family, *deep* in the sea.

He was a goodly fellow who had *one* wish
Of doing something *unique, like NO other fish!*

He wanted to make Allah proud, you see
And prove how *good* a whale he could be!

So once the whale grew *big and strong*
He bid his family *farewell* with a song.

He swam across deep oceans and seas
Looking for ways to help those in *need*.

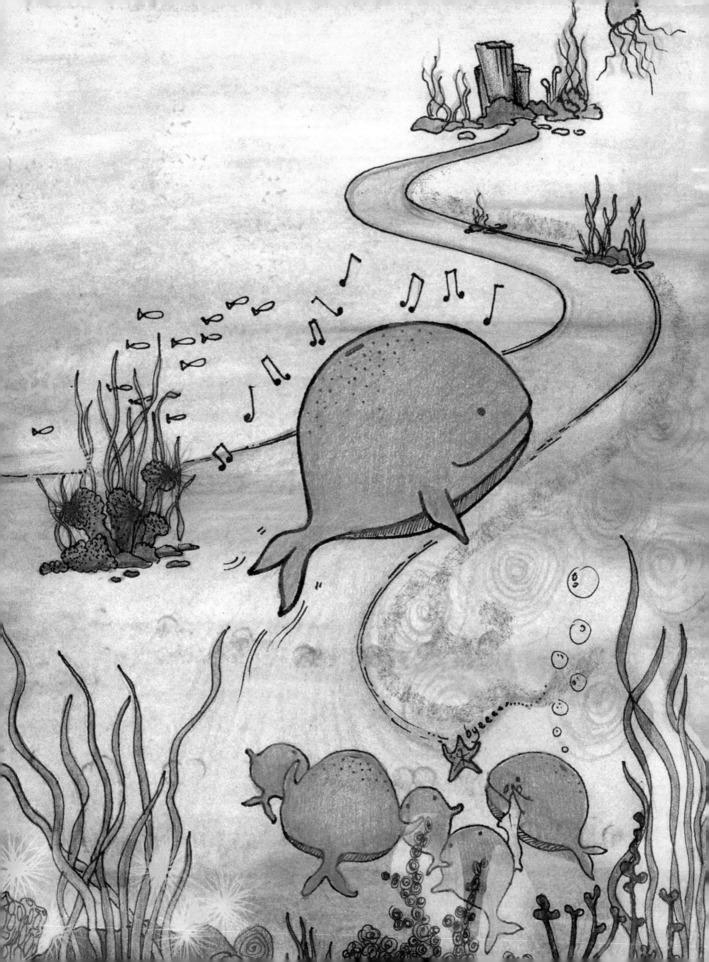

He gave a *helping* hand to *many* along the way
Like saving a dolphin from a *deadly stingray!*

He *even* made friends with *his foe, the giant squid*
Who was quite nice—*when he got to know him a bit!*

Then one night, he wandered *far out to sea*
As he had a *funny* feeling that's where he *needed to be.*

Suddenly, a bolt of lightning hit the sky
Followed by thunder *echoing up high!*

It was the *scariest* storm he had seen in *years*
And he tried his *best to cover his ears!*

He was terrified of thunder and lightning you see
And wanted to swim away—*immediately!*

Suddenly, he spotted a boat up above
Being *thrashed* by the waves, *battered and shoved!*

Then the *poor* whale got *awfully upset*
When he spotted a *MAN* being thrown off the deck!

He watched in *horror* as the poor man fell
Oh what would happen next—*NO ONE could tell!*

Just then, he heard a *voice* in his mind
It was *Allah Almighty, Most Merciful and Kind!*

'Save this man sweet whale, don't fear!
For he is Prophet Yunus, most special and dear!'

The whale trusted *Allah* and *jumped to his call*
Gulping down Prophet Yunus—*arms, legs and all!*

Many *days and nights*, the whale did roam
With Yunus in his belly**,** *so far away from home!*

So night and day the Prophet Yunus *prayed*
'O Allah, forgive me for the mistake that I made!'

Then *finally*, the whale heard Allah's last call
To return the Prophet to land, *once and for all!*

So the goodly whale swam *all* night

Till he reached the shore in the early morning light.

Then *closing his eyes,* he focused on his belly

And *threw up* Prophet Yunus *with some rather slimy jelly!*

Once the Prophet was returned to *dry land*
Saved by Allah's *most marvelous plan,*

The goodly whale, felt thankful and blessed
To have been a BIG part of this *awesome quest!*

So to his family and friends he was *proud* to share
This amazing true story, loved by Muslims *everywhere!*

Dua of the Prophet Yunus (AS)
for relief from hardships

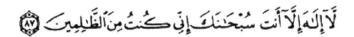

Laa ilaha illa anta, Subhanaka inni kuntum min adhalimeen.

There is none worthy of worship besides You. Glory be to You. Indeed, I have been among the wrongdoers.

Al-Quran Chapter 21, Verse 87

About the Author

Razana was born and raised in Surrey, UK. She has a degree in Law and a diploma in Quranic & Islamic Studies. Writing fun, entertaining children's books with an 'Islamic twist' is her passion! Currently a mother-of-four, she is an advocate of real food, alternative medicine and living a natural lifestyle. When not writing, she can be found experimenting (making a mess) in the kitchen, reading books by Imam Ghazzali, or playing 'rough-and-tumble' with the kids. She is currently pottering on her *next* exciting new title.

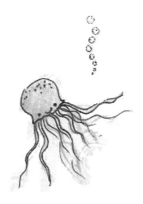

.

Printed in Great Britain
by Amazon